# MEGA BOOKS

# TRACTORS

I0798949

LOUISE PRITCHARD
AND CHRISTIANE GUNZI

Gareth Stevens
PUBLISHING

# BE A SUPER SPOTTER

Study these pictures and look out for them as you read this book. Can you answer the super spotter questions?

**What is this part of?**

**What vegetable is being harvested?**

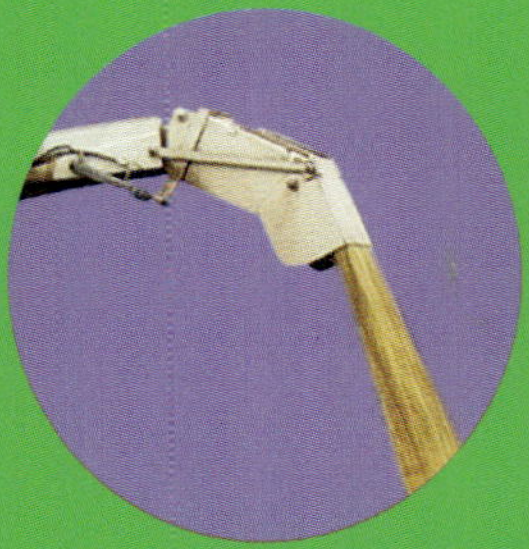

**Why is this important?**

**What does this do?**

**Please visit our website, www.garethstevens.com. For a free color catalog of all our high-quality books, call toll free 1-800-542-2595 or fax 1-877-542-2596.**

Published in 2025 by
**Gareth Stevens Publishing**
2544 Clinton St.
Buffalo, NY 14224



Designer: Paul Calver
Written and edited by: Louise Pritchard and Christiane Gunzi
Editorial assistant: Katy Rayner
Consultant: Peter Love

Thank you to the following companies and individuals for the use of their images:
AGCO Audio Visual Department; Bargam SPA; Case IH; Christian Brocks – European Tractor Pulling Committee; Claas; Clarke Machinery Group Ltd; Clayton Engineering Ltd; Don Carter of Oxbo International Corporation; Horsch Maschinen GmbH; Iain Hawkins with 'Wicked' at STPC Finals 2006, by Lynn Hawkins; Kubota (U.K.) Limited; Kverneland Group; New Holland; Peter Love; Scottish Tractor Pullers Club; Tonutti Spa; TYM International Ltd; www.cfgphoto.com; www.tractorpulling.com

**Cataloging-in-Publication Data**

Names: Pritchard, Louise. | Gunzi, Christiane.
Title: Tractors / by Louise Pritchard and Christiane Gunzi.
Description: Buffalo, NY : Gareth Stevens Publishing, 2025. | Series: Mega books
Identifiers: ISBN 9781482468113 (pbk.) | ISBN 9781482468120 (library bound) | ISBN 9781482468137 (ebook)
Subjects: LCSH: Farm tractors--Juvenile literature. | Agricultural machinery--Juvenile literature.
Classification: LCC S711.P74 2025 | DDC 629.225'2--dc23



Printed in the United States of America

CPSIA compliance information: Batch #CSGS25: For further information contact Gareth Stevens at 1-800-542-2595.

Find us on

# CONTENTS

# FARM TRACTORS

Every farm has a tractor. Most tractors have big wheels and tires so they can drive across fields as well as on roads. Tractors are powerful vehicles. They can pull and push other machines and trailers around the farm.

**Massey Ferguson tractor**

## Massey Ferguson

This Massey Ferguson has a low roof so it can drive inside barns and buildings. Tractors have lots of gears and can go fast or slow.

### Can you point to?

some steps

a wing mirror

a headlight

## John Deere

John Deere tractors are always green and yellow. They have been painted these colors since 1918.

John Deere tractor

**What color is the Massey Ferguson?**

New Holland tractor

## New Holland

This tractor can almost drive itself. A computer inside remembers what the driver did and tells the tractor to do it again, at the touch of a button.

# CRAWLER TRACTORS

A crawler tractor moves along on rubber tracks wrapped around small wheels. The tracks do not squash the soil as much as normal wheels do, so crawler tractors are useful for working on soft, muddy ground.

## Can you point to?

an exhaust

two wheels

a light

## Quadtrac tractor

This red tractor has four tracks. There are two at the front and two at the back. These tracks make the tractor easier to turn. "Quad" means four.

**What are this crawler's tracks made of?**

## Caterpillar crawler

The machines made by Caterpillar are named after a caterpillar because the crawler tracks move like creepy-crawlies!

# OLD TRACTORS

The first farm tractors with engines were made about 140 years ago. They were powered by steam. Lots of old tractors still work today, and people take them to tractor shows.

## Fordson tractor

This Fordson tractor was made over 60 years ago. Its top speed was less than 7 miles (11 km) an hour!

**Massey Ferguson 188**

## Winning prizes

People who own classic old tractors polish them and look after them well. They often enter their tractors in competitions. This Massey Ferguson is about 50 years old.

**Which tractor is blue and orange?**

# A popular tractor

This type of John Deere tractor was first made in 1923. It was popular on farms for 30 years and it had big steel wheels.

John Deere D

Fordson E27N Major

# TRACTORS AND PLOWS

Every autumn, farmers get their fields ready for planting seeds. They use a tractor to pull or push a plow over the fields. The plow turns the soil over so it is ready for planting crops.

## Can you point to?

some numbers

a circle

some letters

**John Deere tractor plowing a field**

## Neat and tidy

Tractors use machines called seed drills to plant seeds in the ground. The seed drills plant the seeds in straight rows.

**Tractor planting with a seed drill**

**Can you see the yellow wheels?**

## Heavy work

This tractor has four-wheel drive. The power goes to all four wheels so that they grip the ground and help the tractor pull the plow along.

**Massey Ferguson tractor plowing**

# CROP SPRAYERS

Farmers use a machine called a sprayer to spray their crops with a special liquid to keep insects away. The liquid is stored in a big tank. The spray comes out of a long arm, called a boom.

**Can you point to?**

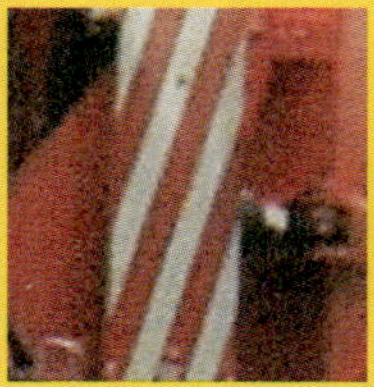

some stripes

a ladder

a logo

## No help needed

This Bargam Mac sprayer is high up off the ground. It has narrow wheels so it does not damage the crops. It sprays as it moves along, and it can carry 1,050 gallons (4,000 l) of liquid in its tank.

## Folded away

This yellow crop sprayer needs a tractor to pull it along. When the sprayer is not being used the boom folds up like wings. It is called a gullwing boom.

John Deere tractor pulling a sprayer along

**Where does all the spray come out?**

Bargam Mac sprayer working in the fields

# COMBINE HARVESTERS

Huge combine harvesters cut the crops of wheat and barley. They separate the stalks from the grains. They put the grains in the grain tank and leave the stalks on the ground. All the stalks dry in the sun and turn into straw!

Claas Lexion combine harvester cutting crops

## Teamwork

A Claas Lexion uses its cutter bar to cut a strip 30 feet (9 m) wide. On very large farms these machines sometimes work in teams.

**Three combine harvesters at work**

# Where does the harvester put the grain?

## Claas Lexion

This is one of the biggest, most popular combine harvesters in the world. It can cut 176 tons (160 mt) of grain and straw in one hour!

# VEGETABLE HARVESTERS

Some harvesters collect potatoes, corn, and other vegetables. They cut down the vegetables, then separate them from the stalks and leaves, and put them into a big tank on the back.

**Can you point to?**

a container

a filter

a rectangle

**Where can you see a green trailer?**

## Cutting corn

This yellow Oxbo harvester travels from field to field like a tractor. Farmers often use these machines to do just one kind of job. This one is collecting corn.

# Beets

This red harvester is collecting sugar beets. It puts the beets in the tank. When the tank is full, they go into a trailer on the tractor. The tractor will take them away.

Harvester loading up a trailer

Tank

# BALERS

Machines called balers collect straw left on the ground after harvesting. Then the balers turn the straw into round or square bales. One baler can pick up the straw, roll it into a bale, wrap it, and drop it in the field to be collected later.

## Wrapping the bales

This tractor has a special machine on the back that wraps up round bales in plastic to keep them dry.

**New Holland tractor pulling a square baler**

## Straw roll

This Massey Ferguson tractor is pulling a round baler. The baler makes a bale, then rolls it out of the back. The driver must be careful because the straw bale could roll down a hill!

**Massey Ferguson baler making bales**

**How many bales of straw can you count?**

## Flat sides

This New Holland baler makes big square bales. The bales are really rectangular, but they are called square. Square bales are easy to stack because they have flat sides.

# FORAGERS

Machines called foragers cut up grass and other plants to make forage. Forage is a name for the dry stems and leaves that horses and cows eat in winter.

**Where is the red tractor?**

## Big jaguar

This Claas Jaguar cuts the plants and chops the stems. It pours the bits through a chute into a trailer on the back of a tractor.

**Claas Jaguar forager**

## Making hay

This tractor is pulling a rake. The rake's wheels have spikes that turn the grass and help it dry into hay.

# GIANT TRACTOR

This is the world's biggest farm tractor. It was built over 30 years ago and works in the United States. Its tank holds 1,000 gallons (3,785 l) of fuel. That's over 70 times more than an average car's tank holds!

## Wow!

The boy below is three years old. See how tiny he is next to this tractor!

# What is this mega tractor called?

## Larger than life

This tractor's name is "Big Bud." It is just over 13 feet (4 m) tall and weighs more than 50 tons (45 mt). It has eight tires and each one is 7.8 feet (2.4 m) high!

# LOADERS AND LIFTERS

Some modern tractors have an arm with a bucket or fork on the end for lifting things. These are very useful on farms because there are lots of things that need lifting.

Caterpillar lifting straw bales

Trac-Lift TM T450

## Little digger

This red tractor is from Japan. It has a small digger bucket on the front for lifting soil, sand, and other light things.

## Tight fit

The tractor below is easy to drive around and can get into small spaces! Its bucket is useful for lifting animal food and bedding.

**Kubota tractor**

**Bucket**

**Which of these tractors is made in Japan?**

## Lifting fork

This yellow tractor has an arm like a forklift truck's arm. The fork on the end can lift and carry big bales of hay or straw.

# RESCUE TRACTORS

Special tractors help to put boats in the sea and take them out again. This Talus sea tractor was specially made to work with the RNLI lifeboats on beaches. It is waterproof so its engine and electronics can work in the sea.

## Working in water

The Talus tractor can drive in up to 5.2 feet (1.6 m) of water. If it broke down in the sea, it could be left on the seabed without any water getting in!

### Can you point to?

a flag

a grille

a lock

## Tractor on tracks

A crawler tractor is useful on sandy beaches because it does not get stuck. The tractor uses a winch to put the boat on a trailer, then pulls it to the boathouse.

**Talus crawler tractor pulling an RNLI lifeboat**

## Where do crawler tractors work?

**Talus MB-4H sea tractor**

## Two ways

This tractor's seat turns around, so the driver can drive the tractor facing forward or backward.

# ROAD BUILDERS

Big, powerful tractors help with roadwork, where they do many different jobs. They pull heavy containers and machines and help to dig and lay new road surfaces.

## Working together

These tractors are making a new road. One tractor is laying down the surface. The other one makes sure the road is level.

**What is this big tractor pulling?**

## Can you point to?

a tube

a triangle

a rectangle

**Fendt tractor pulling a cement carrier**

# Carrying cement

This tractor is pulling a cement carrier. The driver moves a stick called a joystick to make the tractor go faster or slower, and forward or backward.

# RACING TRACTORS

Some amazing tractors enter competitions called tractor pulling. They have to pull a special type of sled along, which gets heavier the farther it is pulled. The tractor that pulls the sled the farthest is the winner.

"Wicked" racing tractor

## Noise and dirt

The tractors make lots of smoke and noise and spray dirt everywhere! Some tractors have extra-large wheels to help them to grip. Others have turbocharged engines.

## What is the driver wearing?

## Doing wheelies

Tractors sometimes do "wheelies," when the two front wheels come off the ground. They have weights to stop them from flipping over.

## Can you point to?

some checks

a driver

a circle

# GLOSSARY

**Bale** – a large bundle of hay, often wrapped in plastic to protect it from wind and rain.

**Crops** – a plant, such as a vegetable or cereal, that is usually grown to provide food for humans or animals.

**Engine** – the part of a machine that turns fuel into power and movement.

**Forage** – sometimes called fodder, it is dried grass or hay for cattle and horses to eat in the winter.

**Gears** – toothed wheels that are used to change the speed of a vehicle.

**Harvest** – the gathering of the crops grown on a farm.

**Plow** – made of metal blades, it is pulled behind a tractor to break up soil and turn it over, ready for planting seeds.

**Tracks** – a wide belt of grooved rubber wrapped around small wheels. Useful for working on soft ground, they won't get stuck like normal wheels.

# INDEX